W9-AKE-298

LIVING GREEN

Durable Goods

WORLD BOOK

a Scott Fetzer company

Chicago

www.worldbookonline.com

Editorial:

Editor in Chief: Paul A. Kobasa
Project Manager: Cassie Mayer
Writer: Brandon Forbes
Researcher: Jacqueline Jasek
Manager, Contracts & Compliance
 (Rights & Permissions): Loranne K. Shields
Indexer: David Pofelski

Graphics and Design:

Associate Director: Sandra M. Dyrlund
Associate Manager, Design: Brenda B. Tropinski
Associate Manager, Photography: Tom Evans
Book design by: Don Di Sante
Contributing Photographs Editors: Kathy Creech,
 Carol Parden

Pre-Press and Manufacturing:

Director: Carma Fazio
Manufacturing Manager: Steve Hueppchen
Production/Technology Manager: Anne Fritzinger

World Book, Inc.
233 N. Michigan Avenue
Chicago, IL 60601
U.S.A.

For information about other World Book publications,
visit our Web site at **http://www.worldbookonline.com**
or call **1-800-WORLDBK (967-5325).**

For information about sales to schools and libraries,
call **1-800-975-3250 (United States)**, or **1-800-837-5365
(Canada).**

Picture Acknowledgments:

Front Cover: © ImageState/Alamy Images
© David Ball, Alamy Images 5; © Mark Boulton, Alamy
Images 51; © Deco/Alamy Images 45; © Chad Ehlers,
Alamy Images 12; © elipascall-willis, Alamy Images 27;
© Chris Gibson, Alamy Images 22; © Francisco Martinez,
Alamy Images 54;© MShields Photos/ Alamy Images 14;
© Alan Myers, Alamy Images 36; © Natural History
Museum/Alamy Images 10; © Chuck Place, Alamy Images
11; © Helene Rogers, Alamy Images 37; © Swerve/Alamy
Images 40; © Jim West, Alamy Images 25; © Wilmar
Photography/Alamy Images 47; © zphoto/Alamy Images
9; AP Wide World 53; AP Wide World 47; © Niagara Inc./
Conserv-A-Store 33, 51; © Don Di Sante 15, 17, 36, 49, 51;
© Nikolaevich, Getty Images 46; © Greenpeace 19;
© Mark Hirsch, Landov 55; © Nestor Bachmann, Landov
44; © Karen Schiely, Lanodv 9; © Matt Faber, Landov 31;
© Reuters/Landov 13; © Mike Blake, Landov 27; © Rio
Tinto, Landov 6; © Jo Yong-Hak, Landov 4; © Shemetov
Maxim, Landov 52; © Matthew Wiley, Masterfile 48;
© Philips Corporation 14; Shutterstock 8, 15, 16, 20, 21, 22,
23, 24, 25, 27, 28, 30, 32 34, 35, 38, 39, 41, 42, 43, 44, 46,
50; Sun Frost 31.

All maps and illustrations are the exclusive property of
World Book, Inc.

Library of Congress Cataloging-in-Publication Data

Durable goods.
  p. cm. — (Living green)
  Includes index.
  Summary: "A guide to living a more environmentally friendly lifestyle by changing general
practices at home and making smart choices when purchasing durable goods. Explores the harmful
impact durable goods can have on the environment through the use of natural resources and
energy. Features include fact boxes, sidebars, activities, glossary, list of recommended reading and
Web sites, and index"—Provided by publisher.
  ISBN 978-0-7166-1408-1
  1. Environmental responsibility—Juvenile literature. 2. Sustainable living—Juvenile literature.
3. Durable goods, Consumer—Juvenile literature. 4. Household supplies—Juvenile literature.
5. Consumer education—Juvenile literature. I. World Book, Inc.
GE195.5.D87 2008
640—dc22
                    2008033264

Living Green
Set ISBN: 978-0-7166-1400-5
Printed in Mexico
1 2 3 4 5 12 11 10 09 08

The text paper of this book contains
a minimum of 10% post-consumer
recovered fiber.

Table of Contents

There is a glossary of terms on pages 60-61. Terms defined in the glossary are in type **that looks like this** on their first appearance in any section.

Introduction

Section Summary

Durable Goods are household items, such as furniture and appliances, that are designed to last a long time.

The manufacture of durable goods requires the use of natural resources and energy. Some durable goods, such as televisions, require energy to work. Global warming is a major issue associated with energy use.

Such durable goods as televisions and other electronics are constantly improved, enticing people to replace older electronics before they wear out.

DURABLE GOODS

Durable goods are objects that surround us in our daily lives. Furniture, carpeting, refrigerators, televisions, and computers are just a few examples of the many durable goods found in the home. Unlike consumable goods, which are used for a short period, durable goods can last several years.

Trash build-up

Though durable goods can last many years, they are often replaced before they wear out. Couches and carpets may be replaced when a living room is redecorated. Televisions, cell phones, and computers are often replaced with newer models. Too often, durable goods are thrown away and buried in **landfills** instead of being recycled. In landfills, such durable goods as home electronics and mattresses are mixed in with other trash and buried.

Many durable goods are made of **synthetic** (human-made) materials, such as plastic. They are not **biodegradable**, so they will take hundreds of years to break down. The amount of trash people throw away is so large that more and more landfills have to be created in order to hold it.

Durable goods often contain chemicals that can harm the environment. When durable goods are buried in landfills, these chemicals can pollute the soil and underground water sources. Some discarded durable goods are taken to **incinerators**, where they are burned. The burning of durable goods can release harmful chemicals into the air.

Use of natural resources

Natural resources are used as materials to make durable goods. Trees are cut down for their wood to make furniture. Metals are mined from the ground and used in electronic components (parts). **Petroleum** (also called oil) is drilled from deep underground and used to make mattress materials and the casings of computers, stereos, and other electronic equipment.

Metal and petroleum are **nonrenewable resources**—that is, they cannot be replenished once they are used up. Petroleum is in very short supply. It is used to make fuel for vehicles and also supplies some of the energy used by factories and electric power plants.

Some natural resources used to make durable goods, such as trees or other plants, are considered **renewable resources** because they can be replenished. For example, new trees can be planted to replace the ones that are cut down. However, it takes many years for trees to grow to their full size, so they are not rapidly renewable.

Water is also considered a renewable resource. However, clean, fresh water is scarce in many parts of the world. Some durable goods, such as dishwashers and clothes washers, require much water to operate.

Durable goods often end up in landfills, where they can add to trash build-up and cause other environmental damage.

Metals, which are used to make such durable goods as electronics, require much energy to manufacture.

Energy use

A huge amount of energy is expended (used up) in the creation, shipment, and sale of durable goods. Most of this energy comes from burning **fossil fuels.** Fossil fuels include oil, coal, and natural gas. These resources are burned to power vehicles and create electricity for homes, factories, and other buildings. Fossil fuels are nonrenewable resources, so they cannot be replenished.

The manufacture of a television shows the large amount of energy required to make a durable good. Televisions are made from a variety of materials, including glass, plastic, metal, and human-made chemicals. The manufacture of each of these materials requires energy. For example, metal must be mined from the earth, a process that requires energy. The metal is then shipped to factories and melted at very high heat, which uses additional energy.

These materials are then shipped to a factory that manufactures televisions. Once the televisions are made, they are shipped to stores, often in another country, where they will be sold. The vehicles used to transport the televisions all burn a form of petroleum for energy.

When we buy and use a television, we become part of its energy consumption. Electronics and other household appliances require energy to work. Energy for our homes comes from power plants, many of which burn fossil fuels to make electricity.

Global warming

Global warming is a major issue associated with energy use. Over the past 200 years, Earth's average surface temperature has continued to increase. Climate change is already endangering many species (kinds) of plants and animals. It could also increase bouts of drought, famine (food shortages that lead to hunger and death), and disease in several parts of the world.

Most scientists agree that human activities, particularly the burning of fossil fuels and the clearing of forests, are the main cause of global warming. When fossil fuels are burned for

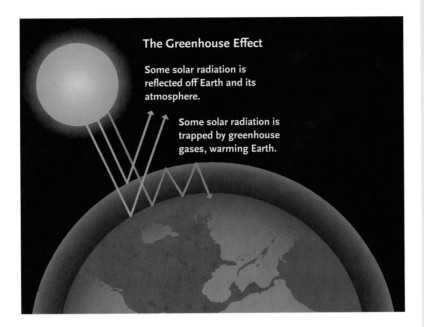

The Greenhouse Effect

Some solar radiation is reflected off Earth and its atmosphere.

Some solar radiation is trapped by greenhouse gases, warming Earth.

Most vehicles, power plants, factories, and other buildings burn fossil fuels for energy. In addition to carbon dioxide gas, the burning of fossil fuels releases many harmful **pollutants,** including **particulates.** These tiny pieces of solid or liquid matter create pollution that stunts the growth of plants, harms the health of humans, and contributes to global warming.

Air pollution from a factory

energy, gases are released into Earth's **atmosphere** that trap the sun's heat, much the same way a greenhouse traps heat. Scientists call this the **greenhouse effect.**

> Greenhouse gases trap the sun's heat, much like a greenhouse.

Carbon dioxide is the main **greenhouse gas** produced by human activities. It is released into the atmosphere when fossil fuels are burned in vehicles and at factories and power plants.

Living green

As evidence for global warming has grown, people around the world have sought ways to reduce their **carbon footprint,** or the amount of carbon dioxide **emissions** their individual actions produce each year. Reducing human impact on the environment requires government action, such as laws that set limits for carbon dioxide emissions, but it also involves individual action.

Living green means making choices that benefit people and the environment. There are many ways to live green, from taking public transportation instead of driving a car to unplugging electronic appliances that are not in use in order to reduce home energy use. Durable goods are a part of everyday life, but the choices we make in how we buy, use, and dispose of durable goods can reduce their environmental impact—and our own carbon footprint.

The Living Room

Section Summary

Furniture that is considered sustainable includes items made from fast-growing plants, recycled materials, or wood from well-managed forests.

Rugs and carpets made from materials that are grown without the use of chemicals are environmentally friendly options for covering your floors.

Electronics that are energy efficient can help reduce energy use in the home.

FURNITURE

Furniture comes in a wide variety of styles suited to different functions. The materials from which furniture is made can determine its environmental impact.

Wood furniture

Much of the furniture found throughout the home is either framed or made out of wood. Although wood is a **renewable resource**, some lumber companies cut down forests faster than they can grow back. Others plant new trees to replace the ones they cut down, but these young forests do not provide the same diverse **habitat** that older forests give to wildlife.

Some furniture factories purchase wood from lumber companies that participate in **deforestation**, the clearing of large areas of forest. Logging and agriculture are the main industries responsible for deforestation, which plays a part in **global warming**. Since trees absorb **carbon dioxide** gas, the removal of trees leads to higher levels of carbon dioxide in the **atmosphere**.

Deforestation is a major threat to tropical forests, such as those found in Central and South America, Southeast Asia, and Africa. Such tree species as mahogany and cedar are threatened because of illegal or otherwise damaging logging practices.

Green furniture

Bamboo furniture is a sustainable alternative to wood furniture.

Those wishing to buy wood furniture with minimal environmental impact can look for items that bear the Forest Stewardship Council (FSC) logo. The FSC is an international organization that **certifies** wood products that come from well-managed forests. The FSC lists products that are made from **sustainable** wood on their Web site (www.certifiedwood.org).

Other sustainble materials for furniture-making include cork and bamboo. These materials are quickly gaining popularity because of their environmental benefits and attractive appearance. Cork is made from the outer bark of an oak tree. Bamboo is a tall, woody grass that can be grown very quickly.

Some of the top furniture designers today are using such recycled materials as rubber, plastic, aluminum, and cardboard to give furniture a unique look. They have also found creative ways to use **reclaimed wood.** Today, you can find home furniture made from old wine barrels, cardboard, railroad ties, or even driftwood.

Green options for furniture are often more expensive than standard items. However, you can still go green on a tight budget by purchasing used furniture at resale shops. This can help prevent natural resources from being used to make new furniture.

Furniture fabrics are often treated with chemicals that can release harmful gases into living areas. Some of these chemicals are used to make the fabric resistant to stains or fire. Others are used in glues that attach the fabric to furniture frames. These chemicals have been shown to be toxic, causing health problems ranging from asthma to cancer.

Chemicals used to treat fabrics are released into a home's air supply through a process called **off-gassing.** To reduce exposure to these chemicals, leave windows open whenever possible for the first few weeks after purchasing new furniture. This will help increase **ventilation** in your home.

Rugs and carpets are often made of synthetic materials that can be harmful to the environment.

RUGS AND CARPETS

Rugs and carpets are often used as decorative items or to give rooms a cozy feel. People rarely give thought to environmental concerns with these items, but what covers the floors in your home can impact your health—and the health of the planet.

Petroleum use

Most rugs and carpets are made of **synthetic** materials, such as nylon, olefin, and polyester, which resist soiling and staining. These materials are made from **petroleum**, a **nonrenewable resource** that is in limited supply.

The manufacture of synthetic fibers releases carbon dioxide, a **greenhouse gas.** In addition, synthetic fibers are not **biodegradable.** They will last many lifetimes when buried in a **landfill.** In 2002, more than 4 billion pounds (1.8 billion kilograms) of carpet were thrown away in the United States, and most of this carpet ended up in landfills.

Toxic chemicals

Formaldehyde (*fawr MAL duh hyd*) glue and other adhesives (sticky substances) are often used to attach carpets to floors. Once carpet is installed, the chemicals in these glues can **evaporate** in a process called off-gassing. These chemicals can off-gas for weeks after carpets have been installed, releasing toxic fumes called **volatile organic compounds (VOC's).** Exposure to VOC's can irritate the lungs, cause headaches, and may lead to more serious health problems.

Allergens

Carpeting is usually not recommended for people with allergies because it collects dust and other particles that are tracked in from outside. Scientists have shown that young children can swallow more than 10 grams (0.35 ounces) of dust a day from carpeting. Much of this dust, if tracked in from the outside, may contain toxic metal particles or even **pesticides** from yard plants.

Many people are allergic to dust mites, tiny animals that live in carpets, rugs, and bedding.

Green rugs and carpets

Up until the 1940's, the majority of rugs and carpets manufactured in the United States were made of wool. Though wool rugs and carpets are more expensive than rugs and carpets made from synthetic fibers, wool is once again gaining popularity due to its green appeal. Unlike synthetic fibers, wool, which comes from sheep, is a renewable resource. Other renewable materials, such as camel's hair, hemp, and seagrass, are also used to make rugs.

Other sustainable materials for carpet- and rug-making include materials made from crops that have been grown organically (without the use of synthetic chemicals). **Organic** cotton is generally considered a sustainable material because it is grown without the use of pesticides and synthetic **fertilizers**, which can pollute soil and bodies of water. Many **environmentalists** recommend purchasing carpets and rugs that are free of other synthetic chemicals, including stain protectors or synthetic dyes.

Understanding which products have the least environmental impact can be a difficult task. However, you can look for items that have been certified by an outside party to help you make purchasing decisions. The Carpet and Rug Institute (CRI) is a U.S.-based organization that awards its "Green Label" to carpets

that meet **emissions** criteria for VOC's and other chemicals. You can also check to see if carpets have met the American National Standards Institute's sustainability standard. (See the "Closer Look" sidebar on this page.)

Some rugs are handcrafted, such as this traditional Mexican rug.

ELECTRONICS

Electronics, such as televisions, stereos, DVD players, and electronic video game systems, supply endless hours of entertainment for many people. However, with increased focus on energy use in the home, many of these items have come to be seen as "energy vampires," sucking power from electrical outlets even when they are turned off.

Many people use electronics for several hours each day, adding to a home's total energy use.

Energy use

Electronics are responsible for much home energy use. In 2006, the U.S. Energy Information Agency reported that electronics consumed more than 25 percent of all household electricity use. That's not surprising, considering that the average U.S. home has the television on nearly seven hours a day.

In the past two decades, advances in digital television have increased the demand for large-screen TV's, such as liquid-crystal display televisions (LCD's). Bigger televisions require more energy to work and have caused television energy use to rise. Plasma televisions, a type of flat-panel, large-screen TV, can use as much energy in one year as some refrigerators.

Most electronics use a large amount of energy even when they are not in use. When these items are turned off, they are actually in standby mode and continue to use energy. In fact, about 40 percent of the energy used by televisions and most other electronics occurs when they are in standby mode.

The "missing" greenhouse gas

The manufacture of all electronics involves materials and processes that can harm the environment in some way. However, some scientists have grown particularly concerned about a chemical used in the manufacture of flat-panel television displays. Nitrogen trifluoride (NF_3) is believed to be more harmful than most greenhouse gases. Scientists estimate that NF_3 is 17,000 times more damaging than carbon dioxide.

Before the invention of the flat-screen television, NF3 was only used in small amounts, such as in the manufacture of lasers and rocket fuels. Because NF3 has not been a major **by-product** of human activities, it is not considered one of the main greenhouse gases. However, as flat-screen TV's have become more popular, the production of NF3 has increased significantly. Some scientists warn that more studies need to be conducted in order to understand how this gas may impact the environment.

E-waste

Some electronics last only a few years, at which point they usually end up in the trash. Almost 2 million tons (1.8 million metric tons) of consumer electronic waste was generated in 2005 alone, and only between 15 to 20 percent of this waste was recycled. The rest made up what is called **e-waste**, the growing amount of electronic trash that is thrown out every year.

E-waste is harmful to the environment in many ways. Most electronic equipment contains metals and such hazardous chemicals as **brominated flame retardants**, which help to prevent them from catching fire. When electronics are buried in landfills, the metals and chemicals can poison soil and nearby water sources. When electronics are burned at an **incinerator**, these substances can release harmful air pollution.

Throwing away electronic equipment also wastes nonrenewable resources, such as the metals inside the components. By throwing out old electronics, millions of tons of metals are being used only once.

The **European Union (EU)** has led the way in **regulating** the disposal of electronics and the materials used to make them. In 2003, it adopted the RoHS (Restriction of Hazardous Substances) Directive, which restricts the use of hazardous chemicals and metals in electronics. The EU also requires that electronics manufacturers put in place recycling programs.

Much of the e-waste in the United States is shipped overseas. Below, a worker at an electronics recycling plant in China sifts through e-waste.

Energy-efficient electronics

Because electronics require natural resources, synthetic materials, and energy to manufacture, they will always cause some harm to the environment, at least for the near future. However, some companies have sought to reduce the environmental impact of electronics by making them more energy efficient.

Philips' Eco TV is an example of how technology can be used to help make televisions more energy efficient. The Eco TV is a flat-screen television that has several energy-saving features, including software that adjusts the screen's backlighting based on the visual content and the room's lighting. This saves the energy that would otherwise be used to make images on the screen brighter. The Eco TV also has a power-consumption monitor that shows the television's energy use.

If you wish to purchase energy-efficient electronics, look for ones that bear the **Energy Star** logo. Energy Star is a joint program of the U.S. **Environmental Protection Agency (EPA)** and the U.S. Department of Energy. It awards certification to electronics and other home appliances that meet their energy-efficiency guidelines. Currently, Energy Star reviews televisions, VCR's, DVD players, and many other home electronics. Overall, electronics that meet Energy Star's standards use as much as 60 percent less energy when in use compared to standard models.

Energy-efficient electronics are often expensive, especially large, flat screen televisions. However, you can cut energy use from televisions considerably by choosing smaller models. Many people prefer their TV's to be as large as possible, but a modest-sized television often requires less energy to work. You can also unplug TV's and electronics that are not in use to save additional energy.

Televisions that bear the Energy Star logo have met their energy efficiency standards for both power mode and standby mode.

Go Green!

Living Green isn't just about the products we buy. It's about the choices we make every day. Here are actions you and your family can take to green your living room:

THE LIVING ROOM

- Repair or re-cover old furniture instead of throwing it out. Upholsterers can replace your furniture's worn-out fabric and give it new life. They can also fix broken frames and tattered cushions.

- When you do need to purchase furniture, shop at resale shops or thrift stores. Buying used furniture reduces the amount of resources needed to make new furniture.

Reupholstering old furniture can make it look new again.

- If you remove carpet from your home, be sure to recycle it. Many carpet installation companies will recycle your old carpets if you ask them to provide this service.

- Unplug the television and other electronics when they are not in use. You can also plug them into a power strip and then turn it off. "Smart" power strips power down automatically when you turn off electronics.

- Reduce the amount of time you spend watching television, as well as the number of TV's in your home, to help **conserve** energy.

Used furniture is often sold at resale shops for discount prices.

The Kitchen

Section Summary

Dishwashers can waste both energy and water. Energy- and water-efficient models help reduce dishwashers' environmental impact. Washing only full loads can help make old dishwashers more efficient.

Refrigerators are the biggest energy users in the kitchen. Choosing energy-efficient refrigerators can reduce kitchen energy use.

Ovens can be the source of much wasted energy. Changing your practices to reduce oven use can help conserve energy.

DISHWASHERS

Once considered a luxury item, dishwashers are now found in many homes. These appliances save time that would be spent scrubbing dishes, but inefficient dishwashers can waste both energy and water.

How they work

Dishwashers contain hoses that connect to hot and cold water pipes in the walls of the kitchen. A water pump propels the water into the dishwasher when it is in use and removes water after a cleaning cycle. Inside the dishwasher, spray arms wash and rinse the dishes. A separate element heats water during the wash cycles and heats air inside the dishwasher during the drying cycle.

Energy use

Appliance use in the home makes up about 20 percent of an average monthly energy bill. Dishwashers use a significant portion of this percentage, mainly because they use hot water for cleaning dishes. Hot water comes from a home's hot water heater, which burns energy to heat the water. The hot water heater also provides the heat needed to dry dishes.

Dishwashers are responsible for much energy and water use in the home.

Water use

Though many dishwashers can save water compared to washing dishes by hand, some models use anywhere between 5 and 15 gallons (19 and 57 liters) of water per load. In the United States, about 300 million gallons (about 1 billion liters) of water are used by dishwashers every day.

Water use results in energy use. Water that goes down the drain is carried in pipes to a **sewage** treatment plant, where the water is cleaned and released into rivers, lakes, and streams. Energy is required to power this cleaning process. (For more information on water use in the home, see pages 28-29.)

Green dishwashers

Energy-efficient dishwashers have features that help reduce their energy and water use. For example, many models have soil sensors, which can tell how dirty dishes are and adjust the amount of water used in a cycle. Some models also have booster burners, which heat only the water needed for a particular load and prevent the hot water heater from overworking.

Consumers who wish to purchase an energy-efficient dishwasher can check the machine's Energy Guide label. This label shows the amount of **kilowatt-hours** used per year and compares the machine's energy use to similar models.

In order to achieve the **Energy Star** rating, dishwashers must use at least 41 percent less energy than the U.S. federal government's minimum standard for energy use. Energy Star models are also more water efficient than standard models.

There are many ways to reduce a dishwasher's energy and water use without replacing it. Running the dishwasher only when it is full maximizes water and energy use. Choosing the no-heat drying option on your dishwasher and letting the dishes air dry can save additional energy. If you don't have a dishwasher, save water by turning off the faucet while you scrub dishes.

GREEN FACT

A **kilowatt** is a unit of power that is used to measure electric power. One kilowatt-hour is a measurement of the work done by one kilowatt in one hour. The Energy Guide label on home appliances shows the average number of kilowatt-hours used by the machine in one year.

Energy Star-rated dishwashers save both energy and water.

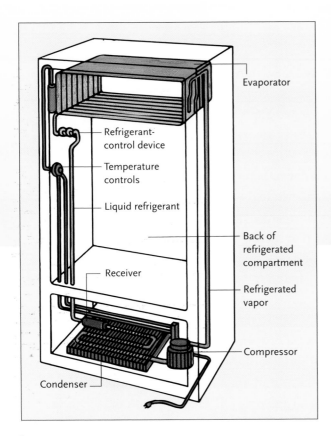

An electric refrigerator circulates a refrigerant through pipes. It is powered by an electrically driven compressor.

Labels on diagram:
- Evaporator
- Refrigerant-control device
- Temperature controls
- Liquid refrigerant
- Back of refrigerated compartment
- Refrigerated vapor
- Receiver
- Compressor
- Condenser

REFRIGERATORS

It is hard to imagine a world without refrigeration. It allows for the travel of food across long distances (in refrigerated compartments aboard trucks, trains, and ships) and for the use and storage of life-saving medical supplies. Refrigerators and freezers in the home keep our food unspoiled and fresh, but this convenience can have hidden environmental costs.

How they work

Home refrigerators contain an electric motor that powers the cycle of refrigeration. This cycle involves changing a **refrigerant** (cooling agent) from a liquid to a gas and back into a liquid. The refrigerant circulates through pipes inside the refrigerator's walls and picks up heat from inside the food compartment. When it does so, the refrigerant changes from a liquid to a gas. The gas then travels outside the food compartment into a unit called the compressor, where it releases the heat and changes back into a liquid. Then the cycle of refrigeration begins again.

Energy use

Refrigerators are the biggest energy users in the kitchen. This energy comes from electric power plants, which usually burn **fossil fuels** for energy. Refrigerator models that were made before the year 2000 can use two to three times as much energy as 21st century models. Because they use so much energy, refrigerators are responsible for large amounts of **carbon dioxide emissions**.

A refrigerator's design can significantly affect its energy use. Side-by-side refrigerator-freezer models often use more energy than top-to-bottom models because they have a bigger freezer door. When the door is opened, warm air enters the freezer, and energy is expended (used) in order to cool it down again. Special features can also increase energy use of a refrigerator. Refrigerators that include icemakers or water dispensers use 15 to 30 percent more energy than standard models.

Energy-efficient refrigerators

Energy-efficient refrigerators can reduce household energy use and save money over time. Though Energy Star-rated refrigerators cost more than standard models, they can save anywhere between $40 and $75 a year in household energy costs. Refrigerators usually last more than 10 years, so these savings add up over time. In general, refrigerators that meet Energy Star's standards use 20 percent less energy than federal standards and 40 percent less energy than models made before 2001.

When purchasing a refrigerator, check the Energy Guide label to find out exactly how much energy the model uses. As with dishwashers, this label shows the rate of kilowatt-hours used per year and compares the machine's energy efficiency to similar models.

There are many ways to save energy without replacing your current refrigerator. Energy Star recommends the following tips for people looking to reduce refrigerator energy use:

- Keep your refrigerator well stocked to minimize its energy use. A full refrigerator does not have to work as hard to stay cool as an empty one, since food retains coolness better than air does.
- Make sure the refrigerator door seals are airtight.
- Minimize the amount of time the refrigerator door stays open.
- Raise the refrigerator temperature to between 35 and 38 °F (1.6 and 3 °C) and the freezer temperature to 0 °F (–17.8 °C).
- Position your refrigerator so that it is not too close to a heat source, such as a dishwasher, an oven, or direct sunlight from a window.
- Make sure there is space between the refrigerator and the wall. This will allow air to circulate around the condenser coils, which will help to keep the refrigerator running efficiently. Vacuuming the coils to keep them clean can also improve a refrigerator's performance.

A greenfreeze refrigerator

The burners and oven on an electric range use electricity to generate heat.

OVENS

Ovens serve many purposes, from roasting and broiling meats to baking breads, casseroles, and cakes. Though ovens increase our cooking options, they can also increase energy use in the kitchen.

How they work

Ovens often come as part of an entire heating unit, called a range. The range has a cooktop with several heating areas, and one or two ovens. Most ranges use either electricity or gas to work. In electric ranges, an electric current generates heat by passing through circular heating units in the oven.

Gas ovens have burners inside them that connect to a pipe that pumps in natural gas. Inside the oven, a small flame called a pilot light stays lighted at all times. When the natural gas enters the oven, the pilot light ignites it, which heats the oven. In both gas and electric ovens, a **thermostat** helps control oven temperature by reacting to temperature changes and adjusting the heat as necessary.

Energy use

Both gas and electric ovens require much energy to work. It is estimated that the average oven uses close to 1,000 kilowatt-hours of energy per year. In the United States, this equals almost 5 percent of the total yearly energy use of the average person.

Energy-efficient ovens

Newer oven models have features that help reduce their energy use. Some gas ovens have ignition systems that turn on the gas without the need for a pilot light. In standard gas ovens, the pilot light has to stay lighted at all times, using gas to do so.

Ovens usually last up to 20 years, so learning to use your oven more efficiently can help save energy. Simple actions, such as not pre-heating the oven whenever possible and turning off the oven for the last few minutes while your food cooks, can help save energy. Using microwaves instead of ovens to reheat food can save additional energy.

Go Green!

Energy-efficient appliances are often more expensive than standard models, but anyone can green the kitchen by following these practices:

THE KITCHEN

- Use pots and pans with tight-fitting lids. This will help bring water to a boil or heat food faster, saving energy that would be spent heating the pot or pan.

- Choose a pot or pan that fits the burner you are using. Using a pot that is even 2 inches (5 centimeters) smaller than the burner can waste up to 40 percent of the energy used to heat the burner.

- If you have a toaster or microwave oven, use one of these appliances whenever possible to reheat food. It is estimated that you can reduce cooking energy by up to 80 percent when you use these small appliances instead of the oven.

- If you wash dishes by hand, remember to run the faucet only while you rinse them. Turning on the faucet at a fraction of full volume will also save water. Use cool water to rinse dishes to save additional energy that would be used to heat the water.

- If your family replaces an old refrigerator, be sure to have it recycled for scrap metal. This will help **conserve** natural resources and keep toxic chemicals in your refrigerator from being released into the environment.

Making simple changes to kitchen practices, such as using the right-sized pot or pan for cooking or using a microwave instead of the oven, can help save energy.

The Bedroom

Section Summary

Mattresses are made from a variety of materials and can contain many human-made chemicals. Mattresses made from natural materials, such as wool, often contain fewer chemicals than standard mattresses.

Cell phones are the largest contributors to electronic trash (e-waste), which can pollute the environment. Recycling old cell phones keeps harmful substances out of the environment. It also helps reduce the amount of natural resources used to make new cell phones.

MATTRESSES

Most people spend about one-third of each day asleep. Making smart choices with mattresses can help make your bedroom a more comfortable—and healthy—environment.

Mattress materials

A mattress consists of three main parts: the quilted outer layer, or casing; the inner core, which usually consists of foam; and spring coils, which provide support. Many of the materials used to make mattresses are derived from **petroleum**, a **nonrenewable resource** that is in very short supply. Polyester, nylon, and poly-urethane (*POL ee YUR uh thayn*) foams are all made from petroleum. The quilted outer layer is commonly made from polyester.

In addition to their environmental effects, petroleum-based materials can cause health problems in humans. Some have been shown to release **volatile organic compounds (VOC's)**, chemicals that can cause respiratory problems and skin irritation.

Some mattress outerlayers are made from a mixture of polyester and cotton, a plant that requires large amounts of water and **pesticides** to grow. Pesticides kill unwanted pests, but they can also damage soil and pollute nearby water sources.

Mattresses are made from a variety of substances, including petroleum.

Mattresses sit on top of a box spring, which helps support the mattress and raises its height. The inside of a box spring commonly contains metal springs and wood planks. As with other wooden household furniture, the wood used inside a box spring may come from logging companies that practice **deforestation**.

Added chemicals

Since 1973, the United States government has set mandatory fire safety standards for mattresses. These standards have caused death rates related to mattress fires to drop dramatically. However, in order to meet these standards, many mattress manufacturers use chemicals that may be toxic to humans.

One such group of chemicals, called **brominated flame retardants (BFR's)**, are used in mattress foams as well as foam furniture, carpets, and electronic appliances. Research on laboratory animals has linked exposure to certain types of BFR's to learning, hearing, and memory impairment, **reproductive** problems, and cancer.

In 2003, the **European Union** outlawed the use of some types of BFR's in mattresses, but they can still be found in many mattresses in the United States. A study in 2003 by the Environmental Working Group, a U.S.-based environmental research organization, found high levels of one type of BFR in humans and harbor seals in the San Francisco Bay area.

Green mattresses

Some specialty companies make mattresses from natural fibers and avoid the use of **synthetic** materials. The mattresses are often made from **organic** cotton, which is harvested without the use of such chemicals as pesticides and synthetic **fertilizers.**

It is difficult to purchase a mattress that is completely free of chemicals. Many organic cotton mattresses are treated with flame-retardant chemicals in order to meet government **regulations.** They may also be treated with synthetic dyes and other chemicals that are added after the cotton is harvested. If you wish to purchase chemical-free bedding, look for organic cotton mattresses that have an organic wool covering. Wool is a natural fire-retardant, so these mattresses are likely to be free of BFR's.

A CLOSER LOOK
The Cost of Cotton

The growth of **conventionally farmed** cotton accounts for 25 percent of all pesticides and synthetic fertilizers used worldwide. When these chemicals reach bodies of water, they can harm fish and other water-living organisms.

Some cotton farmers have switched to organic farming practices, which avoid the use of human-made chemicals. Clothing, linens, and mattresses made from organic cotton are now widely available.

The cotton plant

CELL PHONES

Cell phones have become a convenient part of everyday life. We can use them to talk, send text messages, and even take pictures. Though these devices are very small, they are the largest contributors to the growing stream of electronic trash, or **e-waste**.

How they work

The inside of a cell phone contains many parts, including a circuit board, microphone, speaker, battery, and an antenna. The circuit board is a small board containing electronic parts that are connected to form a circuit. It houses the microprocessor and memory chips, which allow for the basic functioning of the phone.

Many cell phone users replace old phones frequently in order to buy the latest model.

Cell phones transmit and receive messages through radio signals. A network of antennas and other equipment give cell phone users continual reception as they move.

E-waste

Cell phone use has grown steadily since they were introduced in the 1980's. In 2005, the number of cell phone users worldwide reached more than 2 billion and continues to grow. Each year, more and more cell phones are made to keep up with such demand.

Increased cell phone use has led to large amounts of e-waste. In the United States, about 130 million cell phones are thrown away each year. Cell phones contain many metals, including arsenic, nickel, zinc, gold, silver, lead, copper, and cadmium. Metals are nonrenewable resources and take large amounts of energy to mine from the ground. Once buried in **landfills,** the metals from cell phones can seep into the ground, polluting soil and nearby water sources. They can also cause air pollution when cell phones are burned in **incinerators.**

Most cell phones, as well as many other electronics, are treated with brominated flame retardants (BFR's), which help prevent them from catching fire. As with the metals inside cell phones, BFR's can pollute air, soil, and water if cell phones are not disposed of properly.

Recycling cell phones

Currently, there are few green cell phone options. Two pioneering companies in Japan have developed **bio-based** cell phones that **decompose** once they are thrown out. However, these phones are not yet widely available.

The best way to reduce cell phones' environmental impact is by ensuring that old cell phones don't end up in the trash—and eventually in landfills or incinerators. Recycling old cell phones keeps harmful substances out of the environment. It also helps reduce the need to mine more precious metals to make new cell phones.

Many cell phone stores have recycling stations where people can drop off old phones. The U.S. Postal Service provides free, postage-paid envelopes that people can use to send old cell phones, MP3 players, digital cameras, and other small electronics for recycling.

Companies that collect old cell phones determine the condition of the phone and either repair it or recycle its metals. Old cell phones that have minor problems are sent to a **refurbishing** center, where they are repainted and tuned up for reuse. Refurbished cell phones are often resold for a reduced price or given to existing customers when their current phone breaks.

Cell phones that cannot be reused are taken to a **smelter**, where they are melted down to recapture their metals. Some smelters are equipped with special filtering devices that prevent harmful **emissions** from being released during this process. Along with many other precious metals, cell phones contain silver and gold, which are used to make the microchips inside the phone. One ton (0.9 metric tons) of melted-down cell phones produces almost nine pounds (four kilograms) of silver.

At cell phone recycling centers, workers inspect and repair phones so that they can be resold.

A CLOSER LOOK
Cell Phones and Health

Cell phones have been in widespread use for less than 20 years. Because they are relatively new, many scientists fear that the long-term health effects of cell phone use are not yet known. Some studies have shown that a certain type of **radiation** emitted by cell phones may be linked to increased rates of brain cancer. Other studies have shown that prolonged cell phone use has little or no effect on a person's chance of getting cancer.

Until more data has been studied, experts suggest limiting the amount of time you talk on a cell phone. Using a hands-free device to keep cell phones away from your head may help reduce possible health effects.

Go Green!

The bedroom is where we spend a large part of our day, so it's worth taking the time to make it a healthy environment. Below are some tips to greening your bedroom:

Buying used bedroom furniture can save you money and prevent more natural resources from being used to make new furniture.

THE BEDROOM

- Shop at resale stores for such bedroom furniture as tables, chests, and bed frames. This will help prevent natural resources from being used to make new furniture. You can also donate old furniture to resale shops or charitable organizations.

- Consider purchasing linens that are made from hemp or organic cotton. The hemp plant requires few pesticides to grow compared to conventional cotton. Organic cotton is grown without the use of pesticides and other human-made chemicals.

- Make your own drapes using cloth from old sheets or tablecloths. You can also purchase cheap fabrics from the "odds and ends" bin at most fabric stores.

- If you live in an area with a hot climate, consider using a window or ceiling fan instead of an air conditioner. Fans use less energy than air conditioners.

In summer, keep your room cool by drawing the shades during the day to prevent sunlight from heating your bedroom. In winter, leave shades open during the day to heat the room naturally.

If you live in an area with a cold climate, insulate windows so heat does not escape from your room. Old, leaky windows let lots of heat escape, which means that more energy is required to heat your room to a comfortable temperature. You can tape a plastic covering to the inside of window frames during winter. You can also ask a family member to install storm windows.

Be sure to unplug your cell phone charger after the phone has charged. These devices use energy even when they are not in use.

There are many ways to green your bedroom, from taking steps to reduce energy use to choosing clothing and linens made from sustainable materials.

The Bathroom

Section Summary

In many parts of the world, the demand for fresh water is greater than the supply. It is important to cut down on our water use.

Toilets account for the most water use in the home. Purchasing "low-flow" toilets" or making adjustments to old toilets can help reduce water use.

Showers and sinks are places where we often use more water than necessary. Choosing water-efficient showerheads and faucets or purchasing aerator attachments can reduce their water use. Taking quick showers and turning off the faucet while your brush your teeth can save additional water.

Such habits as leaving the faucet running while you brush your teeth can waste large amounts of water over time.

WATER USE

When it comes to water use, the United States is more wasteful than any other country. Each day, the average person in the United States uses around 125 gallons (473 liters) of water in the bathroom alone. Being smart about water use in the bathroom can help save thousands of gallons of water each year.

Dwindling freshwater supplies

In many parts of the world, drought, agriculture, population increase, and poor water **conservation** habits have drained freshwater supplies. This is especially true in such dry, desert areas as the southwestern United States, where there are limited freshwater sources. More than 25 percent of Southern California's water supply is usually imported from the Colorado River. However, a prolonged drought in the Colorado River Basin has reduced this number by 50 percent.

Scientists believe that **global warming** is increasing the frequency and severity of droughts in many parts of the world. In Murcia, a region of southeastern Spain, drought, the planting of crops that need to be heavily irrigated, and increasing numbers of such water-intensive developments as golf courses and resorts have all contributed to severe water shortages.

Freshwater supplies can become even more limited by pollution. While **industrialized countries** have well-developed systems for treating water, many less developed countries lack reliable sources of fresh, clean water. In fact, obtaining potable (usable) drinking water is a pressing challenge for many of the 6.6 billion people on Earth. According to the World Health Organization, 18 percent of the world's population lacks access to safe drinking water.

The lack of fresh water is an especially large problem in parts of Africa, although water pollution affects people around the world. In 2008, more than 1,250 people in the United States became ill after eating jalapeños that had been irrigated with water contaminated with a type of bacteria that can cause serious intestinal distress.

Water and energy use

Every time we use water, we also use energy. Water that goes down our drains must be cleaned and purified at a **sewage** treatment plant. Electric power plants supply this energy. Most electric power plants burn **fossil fuels**, releasing **carbon dioxide** and other **pollutants** into the **atmosphere.**

Using hot water adds to this energy use. Hot water pipes connect to a hot water heater in the basement. Energy is required to run the hot water heater.

Drainage pipes in many homes connect to sewers, which send wastewater to treatment plants.

A CLOSER LOOK
Electric Power Plants

Water is an important part of generating electricity at coal-burning power plants. Coal is burned to heat water and create steam. The force of the steam turns a large, wheellike object called a **turbine.** The turning of the turbine generates electric power.

Scientists estimate that for every **kilowatt hour** of energy created by a coal-burning power plant, about half a gallon (about 2 liters) of water is lost. Thus, while conserving water can help save energy, the reverse is also true—conserving energy can help save water.

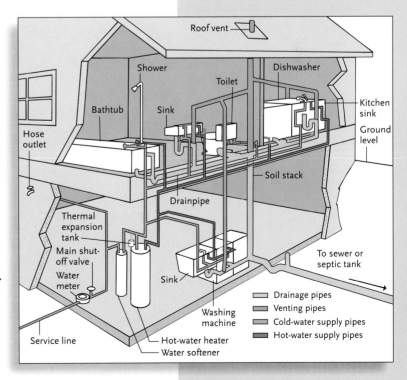

Roof vent

Shower

Toilet

Dishwasher

Bathtub

Sink

Kitchen sink

Ground level

Hose outlet

Soil stack

Drainpipe

Thermal expansion tank

Main shut-off valve

Water meter

Sink

To sewer or septic tank

Washing machine

Service line

Hot-water heater

Water softener

☐ Drainage pipes
☐ Venting pipes
☐ Cold-water supply pipes
☐ Hot-water supply pipes

Older toilets can use up to three times as much water as some "low-flow" models.

TOILETS

Before the invention of the toilet and indoor plumbing, humans had to go outside to heed nature's call. Toilets are one of the many conveniences of modern life, but they also account for the most water use in the home. Choosing water-efficient toilets—or making homemade adjustments to your current toilet—can help reduce water use in the bathroom. (For information on how to make a water-saving toilet device, see the activity on page 56.)

How they work

A toilet consists of a bowl and a tank, both of which are filled with water. When the toilet is not being flushed, a stopper ball or a flapper covers an opening at the bottom of the tank, preventing water from flowing out. When the toilet is flushed, the action of pushing down on the handle lifts the stopper ball or flapper, allowing water to rapidly flow into the bowl. The force of the rapidly moving water causes the water and waste products to empty into a pipe that eventually connects with larger sewage pipes. The toilet then refills with water.

Water use

In the United States, toilets use more than 5 billion gallons (19 billion liters) of water each year—about 40 percent of the total home water use. Around the world, an estimated 27 percent of the water used by each home goes toward toilet use.

Many countries mandate (require) that new toilets must use less than 2 gallons (7.6 liters) of water per flush. However, older toilets can use anywhere from 3 to 7 gallons (11 to 26.5 liters) of water per flush. Leaks in the toilet tank can cause hundreds of gallons of excess water to flow into sewers each month.

High-efficiency toilets

High-efficiency toilets, commonly called low-flow toilets, first became available in North America in the 1990's, but they did not have the same flushing power as standard models. However, big

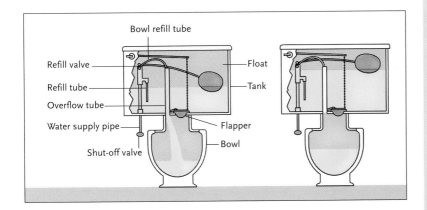

improvements have since been made, and consumer tests have shown that most water-efficient toilets now perform as well as standard toilets.

The **Environmental Protection Agency's (EPA)** WaterSense Label identifies toilets that meet the EPA's guidelines for efficiency and performance. The EPA estimates that WaterSense models save approximately 4,000 gallons (15,140 liters) of water per year compared to standard toilets. These models are often more expensive than standard toilets, but they can save an average household more than $90 per year in water utility bills and $2,000 over the **life span** of the toilet.

It is also important to check that older toilets are functioning properly. Get your toilet fixed if it has a leak or runs for several minutes after you flush it.

When a toilet refills, the float rises with the level of the water in the tank (left). When the tank and bowl are full, the float causes the refill valve to close over the water supply pipe (right) and stop the flow of water.

Some water-saving toilets, such as this one, use waste water from the sink for flushing.

A CLOSER LOOK
Composting Toilets

Those seeking to minimize water use from the toilet have purchased what some are calling an "indoor outhouse." **Composting** toilets use little or no water to contain and control waste products, and are slowly gaining popularity for residential use.

While standard toilets use the force of water to flush away waste into pipes, composting toilets release waste into a chamber inside the toilet. There, moisture is removed from the waste, which breaks down naturally over time. A fan inside the toilet creates a draft, which in turn pulls air from the toilet into a vent. This helps to create an odor-free environment. After several weeks, the waste breaks down into a rich **fertilizer** that can be used on non-edible yard plants.

SHOWERS AND SINKS

While there is only so much we can do to reduce toilet use, we often spend more time in the shower or at the bathroom sink than needed. Shortening the length of our daily bathroom rituals and switching to water-efficient fixtures are two ways to reduce our water use.

Water use

Most of us take for granted the convenience modern plumbing affords. All we have to do is turn the knob on our shower or sink faucet and out comes a gushing stream of water. However, this magic flow of water accounts for much of our water use in the bathroom. Each year in the United States, faucet use accounts for more than 1 trillion gallons (3.785 trillion liters) of home water consumption. Some of this water is used unnecessarily, such as when we leave the water running while brushing our teeth or washing our face.

Showering or taking a bath accounts for a large amount of indoor water use. An average bathtub takes 70 gallons (265 liters) of water to fill. Taking a short shower uses less water than taking a bath, but leaky showerheads can account for much wasted water. Standard showerheads also generally use more water than necessary. Some homes have multiple-head showers that can use up to 80 gallons (303 liters) of water a minute.

Changing bathroom practices, such as taking quick showers and minimizing water use from sinks, can help reduce overall water consumption.

Energy use

Since heating water takes energy, such practices as taking frequent hot baths or long, hot showers can waste energy. Hot water heaters use natural gas or electricity from power plants to heat water. Every year, carbon dioxide **emissions** from coal-burning power plants can reach in the thousands of pounds just from the average family's shower use.

Many household faucets use a device called a washer to control the flow of water to the sink.

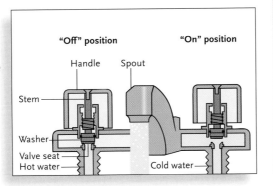

"Off" position   "On" position

Handle   Spout

Stem

Washer

Valve seat

Hot water   Cold water

Green bathroom fixtures

Faucets that meet the EPA's WaterSense standards can reduce a sink's water flow by 30 percent and save more than 500 gallons (1,893 liters) of water a year. WaterSense does not currently have standards for showerheads, but new showerheads are **regulated** to use no more than 2.5 gallons (9.5 liters) of water per minute. Switching to a new showerhead can reduce bathroom water use and your electric bill by 50 percent.

Aerators, attachments that mix air into the water stream to reduce the actual amount of water being used, cost as little as $5 and can be added to existing faucets and showerheads to make them more water-efficient. Though aerators use less water, the mixing of air into the water flow maintains the pressure and fullness of the shower spray.

Some water-efficient homes have installed systems that store sink waste water in a tank underneath the sink. The tank connects to the toilet, which uses the wastewater when the toilet is flushed. Such systems are expensive to purchase, but they can reduce home water use considerably. According to WaterSaver Technologies, a manufacturer of such a system in the United States, using sink waste water for the toilet can reduce water usage in a two-person household by about 5,000 gallons (18,900 liters) a year.

Low-flow showerheads can help reduce our overall water consumption in the bathroom.

Go Green!

Reducing water and energy consumption are the first steps toward greening the bathroom. Using environmentally friendly personal care and bathroom products are additional steps you can take. Below are a few simple ways to go green:

To save water and energy, use towels several times before washing them.

THE BATHROOM

- To cut down on unnecessary water use, throw non-waste items in the trash rather than flushing them down the toilet.

- Take two minutes off the amount of time you usually spend in the shower to save water. You can use a kitchen timer to help you keep track of the amount of time you spend in the shower.

- Turn off the faucet while brushing your teeth, washing your face, or shaving.

When taking a bath, be sure to plug the drain before you start running the water. You can waste countless gallons of water a year if you run the bath faucet before you plug the drain.

Whenever possible, let your hair dry naturally instead of using a hair dryer. This will help reduce energy use in the bathroom.

Use a shower curtain liner made from cloth material. Cloth liners can be washed when they get dirty. They are also made from a **renewable resource** (cotton), unlike plastic shower curtain liners, which are made from **petroleum.**

Reduce the amount of **disposable** personal-care products you use in the bathroom. Whenever possible, purchase refillable soaps and toiletries.

To make an old toilet use less water, fill a small container with stones and place it in your toilet tank. This will raise the water level in the tank, reducing the amount of water needed when the tank refills after flushing. (See the activity on page 56.)

To check your toilet for leaks, pour a small amount of food coloring into the toilet's tank. If the color appears in the toilet bowl before you flush, you know that you have a leak to fix. (See the activity on page 57.)

There are many ways to green your bathroom, from buying refillable liquid soap containers to turning off the faucet while you brush your teeth.

The Laundry Room

Section Summary

Washing machines consume much water and energy. Purchasing energy-efficient washing machines can help reduce household energy use. Using cold-water cycles can further reduce energy use.

Clothes dryers also use large amounts of energy. Some dryers have features that reduce their energy use, but line-drying clothes is the greenest option.

Older top-loading washing machines require more water than front-loading models.

WASHING MACHINES

Not too long ago, people throughout the world spent much time doing their laundry by hand. Some soaked their clothes in streams and then beat them with rocks to get the dirt out. Later, people scrubbed their laundry on washboards. Today, washing machines make it much easier to do laundry, but this convenience adds to our total energy and water use in the home.

How they work

Washing machines contain hoses that connect to hot and cold water pipes. Controls allow the user to select the length of washing and rinsing time. The user can also choose the amount of water that enters the basket at the center of the machine, where the clothes are placed. Once the clothes are washed and rinsed inside the basket, the washing machine spins rapidly to remove water from them. Water is then sent to the outer rim of the basket, where it is pumped out of the machine through a drain hose.

Water use

After toilets, washing machines are the second largest users of water in the home. Some experts estimate that washing machines account for anywhere between 15 and 22 percent of a home's total water use each year. In the United States, about 4.5 billion gallons (17 billion liters) of water are used every year just to wash clothes.

Energy use

Washing machines also consume much energy, most of which is used to heat the water for the hot and warm wash cycles. The cost of heating water for use in a washing machine can account for up to 10 percent of a home's monthly energy bill. Energy in the home comes from electric power plants, which release the **carbon dioxide** and other **pollutants** into the air.

Green washing machines

Within the past 20 years, energy- and water-efficient washing machines have become increasingly available. While standard washing machines use about 40 gallons (151 liters) of water per load, water-efficient models can use less than 25 gallons (95 liters) of water for the same cycle. The machine's design can impact its water use. Front-loading washers can reduce water consumption by up to 25 percent compared to top-loading models. This is because they do not have to fill up completely with water.

Newer washing machines have many water- and energy-saving features, such as electronic controls that automatically adjust the water levels according to the size of the load, and energy-**conserving** options for the wash and spin cycles. They also have higher spin cycles that remove more water from clothes, saving energy that would be used by the clothes dryer.

Many governments have set standards for water use in washing machines. In the United States, washing machines must use only between 18 and 25 gallons (68 and 95 liters) of water per load, which can save about 7,000 gallons (26,500 liters) of water a year per household compared to older models. Newer machines also use 37 percent less energy.

Energy Star rates washing machines on both their energy and water consumption. The Modified Energy Factor (MEF) is a measure of the total energy used by the machine, including the energy used to heat the water. The Water Factor (WF) shows the number of gallons of water needed for each cubic foot of laundry.

Consumers can check the machine's Energy Guide label to see the number of **kilowatt-hours** used per year.

Many washing machines include energy- and water-saving features.

A CLOSER LOOK
Super-Efficient Home Appliance Initiative

In 1997, the Consortium for Energy Efficiency, Inc. (CEE), a U.S.-based organization that works to develop efficiency specifications, launched the Super-Efficient Home Appliance Initiative (SEHA). This national program includes efficiency guidelines for many household appliances, including dishwashers, refrigerators, air conditioners, and clothes washers. CEE's guidelines for appliances are often similar to Energy Star's standards, though many are set at the highest end of the energy-efficiency scale.

Energy-efficient clothes dryers can help reduce yearly carbon dioxide emissions from homes.

CLOTHES DRYERS

Clothes dryers can save hours compared to air-drying clothing. While convenient, dryers use large amounts of energy, adding millions of pounds of carbon dioxide to the **atmosphere** every year.

How they work

A clothes dryer speeds the **evaporation** of water from clothing by applying hot air. A gas or electric heating element heats the air inside the dryer. The blower keeps the air circulating, and the tumbler (rotating drum) keeps the pieces of clothing separate, enabling air to move between them. Water vapor removed from the clothing escapes the dryer through a vent.

The drying time and temperature settings can be adjusted by the operator. Drying clothes for too long or at too high a temperature can waste energy.

Energy use

In the United States, yearly electricity use from dryers equals more than 66 billion kilowatt-hours. All of this energy consumption contributes to **greenhouse gas emissions**. Each year, the average U.S. household is responsible for more than 2,000 pounds (907 kilograms) of carbon dioxide emissions from dryer use.

Green dryers

Unlike washing machines, clothes dryers are not reviewed by the Energy Star program. However, many models have features that make them more energy efficient. Some new dryers come with moisture sensors that detect when clothing is dry, at which point the dryer automatically turns off. Some dryers have an air-dry feature, which pulls air into the machine to dry clothes without using heat.

Gas dryers are considered by some experts to be more environmentally friendly than electric dryers. Though they are powered by a **fossil fuel** (natural gas), gas dryers are cheaper to run than electric dryers, save wear and tear on clothes, and can cut a dryer's yearly carbon dioxide emissions by 40 percent.

Go Green!

There are many additional ways to green your laundry room, some of which are listed below:

THE LAUNDRY ROOM

🍃 Reducing the amount of laundry you do is one of the simplest ways to reduce energy and water use in the home. Hang bathroom towels to air dry after use in order to prolong the amount of time you can use them before they need to be washed. Wash such items as pants and sweaters only when they are dirty.

🍃 To save energy when you do wash your clothes, use cold water for all wash cycles. Hot water cycles use energy to heat the water.

🍃 Wash full loads to maximize the amount of laundry per gallon of water used. However, be careful not to overload your washer, as this can damage the machine and cause it to use additional energy.

🍃 On sunny days, line-dry clothing outside to save energy. Using a clothesline to dry your laundry can save you up to $85 dollars a year in energy costs.

🍃 Buy large packages of concentrated detergent to cut down on packaging trash.

🍃 Remove the lint (fluffy pieces of material) that catches in the lint screen after every load to maximize the machine's energy efficiency. Keeping the dryer free of lint can save you 5 percent on your energy bill every year.

🍃 Use auto-dry settings if your dryer has them. These can save energy and reduce the risk of clothing shrinkage, static electricity, and reduce the wear and tear on your clothes caused by over-drying.

🍃 Placing your dryer in a heated space can save you even more energy each month. If the space is already warm, clothes will not take as long to dry.

Line-drying clothing on sunny days saves energy that would be used by a clothes dryer.

The Office

Section Summary

Computers are often left on even when they are not in use, a practice that wastes energy. Choosing energy-efficient computers and turning off computers that are not in use can reduce their energy consumption. Recycling old computers can also help reduce their environmental impact.

Without computers and the Internet, modern civilization would grind to a halt.

COMPUTERS

Computers and the Internet have revolutionized the way we live. We can use computers to write, look up information, store images and music, communicate with people across the world through live video, and play games. While computers are a vital part of our everyday lives, they contribute to our total energy consumption and produce a significant amount of **e-waste**, both of which are growing environmental concerns.

How they work

Personal computers, also called PC's, come in two types: desktops, where the computer, monitor, keyboard, and mouse are separate units; or laptops, which contain all of the components in one compact package.

PC's contain many internal components. One of the main components is a large circuit board called the motherboard, which connects to every internal component. Located on top of the motherboard are memory chips, which store information and processing instructions; and storage devices, which hold data.

The motherboard also houses the central processing unit (CPU), also called the microprocessor. The CPU functions as the "brain" of the computer, where all information is processed.

The user enters information into a computer through input devices, such as the keyboard and mouse. When an electric current passes through the circuit board, units of information are passed from circuit to circuit. The information is then displayed on the computer monitor.

Energy use

As with all household appliances, computers use electrical energy that is generated at power plants, most of which burn **fossil fuels**. The burning of fossil fuels depletes Earth's supply of **nonrenewable resources**. It also releases **carbon dioxide** into the **atmosphere**.

Because computer use is so widespread, it accounts for a significant amount of energy use. Many people around the world spend much of their day working on a computer. After a long day at work or school, they may go home and spend even more time on the computer, writing e-mails or surfing the Internet. Worldwide computer use adds up to a total of $250 billion dollars in energy costs. Laptops and desktops with flat-screen monitors are more energy efficient than standard desktop models, but their energy use adds up over time.

Much of a computer's energy consumption happens when it is left on but not in use. According to some estimates, only about 15 percent of the energy consumed by computer users worldwide is spent on actual computing time. The other 85 percent of that power is used while computers are not even in use, such as when they are left on overnight.

Many people leave computers on all day, even when they are not in use.

Computer materials

Computers are made from many different materials, all of which have some environmental impact. The casing, or outer body of the computer, is often made of plastic. As you have read, plastic is derived from **petroleum**, a valuable nonrenewable resource.

The components inside a computer are made of plastics, chemicals, metals, and other materials. Though many computer components are incredibly small, they take large amounts of resources to make. According to National Geographic's *Green Guide* magazine, the manufacture of one silicon wafer, the main substance inside computer chips, takes 20 pounds (9 kilograms) of chemicals, 285 **kilowatt-hours** of electricity, more than 2,275 gallons (8,612 liters) of water, and more than 22 cubic feet (6.7 cubic meters) of hazardous gases.

Computer circuit boards are made of many materials, including metal.

E-waste

Like cell phones and other household electronics, computers are a major contributor to e-waste. With upgraded versions of computers coming out all the time, many old computers end up stored in closets or basements. According to some estimates, more than 75 percent of all computers in the United States are not used because they are out of date. The rest are simply thrown out. Many of these computers end up in **landfills**, where their toxic metals and chemicals can seep into soil and pollute nearby water sources.

Many computer companies have established programs that allow customers to return old computers when customers upgrade to a new machine. Some will even take computers that are made by a different company. The Computer Takeback Campaign is a U.S.-based non-profit organization that compares computer companies' takeback programs on their Web site (www.computertakeback.com).

There are also computer-recycling companies that take your computer off your hands for free. However, some of these companies ship e-waste to countries where e-waste recycling practices have created health and environmental problems.

GREEN FACT

In July 2008, the European Union restricted the use of six hazardous materials commonly used in the manufacture of electronic equipment. These include lead, mercury, a cancer-causing form of chromium, cadmium, and two different flame retardants.

The amount of e-waste from computers and other electronics continues to grow each year.

About 70 percent of all discarded computers and phones are shipped to China, where workers remove circuit boards and melt them down so the individual components can be resold. Burning circuit boards, which contain **heavy metals**, releases toxic fumes. Recent studies in China have shown the effects of burning computer parts. In 2008, a scientist at Hong Kong Baptist University found that the dust samples near computer recycling sites contained 370 times more lead than areas 18.6 miles (30 kilometers) away from the sites.

In many countries, recycling companies remove the valuable parts of a computer and throw away the remaining parts. However, some recycling companies separate a computer's parts in a safe manner and dispose of unusable toxic materials appropriately. Many of these companies also save certain computer parts to be re-used in other goods, such as clocks.

If you do get a new computer, be sure to recycle your old one. Find out if your computer company takes back old computers, or bring your old computer to an e-waste recycling company. Research their methods of recycling e-waste, such as whether they ship e-waste to other countries, the methods they use to process it, and the health and safety of the workers who sort the e-waste.

Green computing

The **Environmental Protection Agency's (EPA) Energy Star** program includes separate energy-efficiency standards for desktop computers, monitors, and laptop computers. The EPA bases its standards on the amount of energy used during standby and sleep modes and while computers are in use. Energy Star anticipates that their efficiency standards will save personal computer users and businesses a total of $1.8 billion in energy costs over a five-year period.

Unfortunately, computers are expensive to buy and they tend to become outdated within a matter of years. However, you can take simple steps to keep an old computer in use for as long as possible. One way to do so is by purchasing software and hardware upgrades. Software includes programs that are run on computers, such as word processing programs. Hardware includes the physical parts of your computer, such as the hard drive and

Laptop computers are more energy efficient than desktop models.

memory chips. If your computer does not have enough memory, the best graphics, or the right number of drives, look into getting it upgraded at a computer repair shop. These repairs or upgrades can be less expensive than buying a new computer.

In order to make your current computer more energy efficient, change its power management settings so that your computer goes into standby or sleep mode after five minutes. Though you should always turn off your computer when it is not in use, it is sometimes more practical to leave the computer on if you are only going to be away from it for a few minutes. Most computers have a standby or sleep mode that uses a very small amount of power when the computer is not in use.

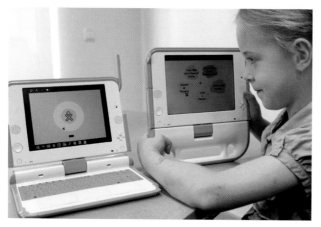

These computers were designed as part of the One Laptop per Child initiative. The initiative aims to provide an affordable, durable computer for educational use around the world.

Go Green!

Many people spend several hours on a computer each day for school, work, or general information gathering. However, there are still ways we can green our computing practices. Here are additional tips to greening the office:

THE OFFICE

- Remember to shut down your computer when you are not using it. It is a myth that leaving a computer on all the of time is better for the computer than shutting it down every night.

Old computers and other electronics can be taken to recycling stations, such as this one in Sweden.

- If you cannot find a computer recycling station in your community and your old computer works well, consider donating it to a school or charity. Your donation will give others access to a computer for educational purposes. It will also keep the computer out of the trash.

- Green computing also involves green printing. Be sure to turn off your printer, copier, or scanner after every use or put it into standby or sleep mode.

- Only print out documents that you cannot read on a computer screen. This will help save energy, paper, and ink.

- Keep a recycling bin in the office to recycle used computer paper. You can also use old printouts as scrap paper.

- Change your computer's printer settings to print on both sides of paper.

- Find out if your printer company accepts old ink cartridges for recycling. Many companies provide postage-paid labels that can be used to send back used ink cartridges.

The Yard

Section Summary

Grills commonly used in yards release carbon dioxide into the atmosphere. Electric grills are a more environmentally friendly alternative to charcoal and propane grills. Solar grills, which use heat energy from the sun, release no pollutants.

Mowers that use gasoline release large amounts of pollution. Electric mowers, battery-powered motors, and reel mowers are green alternatives to these mowers.

Charcoal grills are responsible for surprisingly large amounts of carbon dioxide emissions each year.

GRILLS

Grilling is a popular summertime activity that is often as much about enjoying the outdoors as it is about cooking food. However, grills can account for surprisingly large amounts of pollution.

How grills work

One of the most common types of grill is the **charcoal** grill. Charcoal is made from wood that has been heated to remove its water content. With a charcoal grill, the operator simply lights the charcoal, which burns underneath the cooking surface to produce heat.

Another popular choice for grilling is the gas grill, which burns either natural gas or liquid **propane** for heat. Gas grills have one or two burners. Natural gas or propane is pumped into the burner through a hose that connects to a tank of gas underneath the grill. The propane or natural gas mixes with oxygen inside the burner. The operator then ignites the gas inside the burner either with a match or by pushing the igniter button, which creates a spark. The heat from the burner then enters the body of the grill underneath the cooking surface.

Carbon dioxide emissions

Charcoal grills release large amounts of **carbon dioxide** gas into the **atmosphere.** This is because charcoal is made up of 80 to 90 percent of the chemical element carbon. When carbon is burned, it is released into the air, where it mixes with oxygen and forms carbon dioxide. (Carbon dioxide is made up of one atom of carbon and two atoms of oxygen.)

Gas grills are responsible for fewer carbon dioxide **emissions** than charcoal, but they do rely on **fossil fuels** for heating.

Green grilling

Electric grills are considered a green alternative to charcoal and gas grills. They release 91 percent fewer carbon dioxide emissions than a charcoal grill and 21 percent fewer emissions than a gas grill. However, these grills use electricity to heat their cooking surfaces, so they are responsible for some carbon dioxide emissions that are released by power plants.

Solar-powered grills are the most environmentally friendly option for grilling. These grills use metal covered with a mirror to focus heat from the sun into a central cooking area. Solar grills are emissions-free and cook just as well as gas or charcoal grills. However, solar grills don't work well on cloudy days.

Some people prefer the smoked taste that charcoal-burning grills give to food and are reluctant to make the switch to a more environmentally friendly grill. If you do use charcoal to grill your food, it is best to use charcoal products that come from hardwood trees. This type of charcoal is denser than standard charcoal and takes longer to burn. Low-smoke varieties of charcoal that come from wood scraps from furniture manufacturers are another green option.

Electric grills (top) use electricity for grilling. Solar grills (bottom) use heat from the sun to power cooking.

Gasoline-powered mowers release carbon dioxide and other pollutants into the atmosphere.

LAWN MOWERS

Every spring, the hum of lawn mowers trimming yard spaces sounds once again. Lawn mowers help keep yards looking well-groomed, but they also release large amounts of carbon dioxide emissions and other **pollutants.**

How they work

Lawn mowers contain a blade that rotates around a vertical or horizontal axis. Push mowers, which contain a gasoline engine to power the blade, are the most commonly used lawn mower for small yard spaces. Riding lawn mowers, in which the user sits in a chair on top of the mower, are gasoline-powered mowers that are sometimes used for large yards.

Carbon dioxide build-up

Both push and riding mowers require much gasoline to run. Gasoline, a fossil fuel that comes from **petroleum**, releases carbon dioxide into the atmosphere when it is burned. It is estimated that more than 720 million gallons (2.7 billion liters) of gasoline are burned every year to power lawn mowers across North America. Older push mowers can release the same amount of carbon dioxide in one hour as 11 cars; a riding lawn mower can release as much carbon dioxide as 34 cars.

Lawn mowers release more harmful emissions than cars because they have very basic engines. Since 1973, all cars in the United States have been fitted with **catalytic converters**, devices that reduce emissions from gasoline engines. Most lawn mower engines do not contain this device.

Gasoline-powered lawn mowers also pollute the environment through accidental spills when a mower is refueled. According to the U.S. **Environmental Protection Agency (EPA)**, 17 million gallons (64,352,000 liters) of fuel are spilled each year when people refuel lawn equipment. Gasoline is toxic to the environment. If it spills onto the ground, it can seep into the soil and may eventually end up in an underground water source.

Smog

Lawn mower emissions also contain **carbon monoxide**, a poisonous, colorless, odorless gas that contributes to the build-up of **smog**. Smog is a type of air pollution that is created by emissions from gasoline-burning engines. It can cause such breathing problems as asthma and has been linked to heart disease and strokes. In 2006, a scientific study showed that for every gallon of gasoline burned, a lawn mower releases 93 times more smog emissions than a car.

Green lawn mowers

Those wishing to give up gasoline-powered mowers needn't do so at the expense of a neatly trimmed lawn. Electric-powered mowers save around 6 pounds (2.7 kilograms) of carbon dioxide emissions per use compared to gasoline-powered mowers. They also release minimal carbon monoxide emissions, are much quieter than gasoline-powered mowers, and generally have lower maintenance costs.

Some electric mowers are battery powered, allowing for cordless mowing. After use, the mower is plugged into an electrical outlet to recharge its batteries. Most models can mow for about an hour before they need to be recharged. These electric mowers are best for larger lawns, where a long cord can get in the way of mowing.

The greenest mower available is a reel mower. Reel mowers are hand-pushed and use no electricity or gas. They contain sharp blades that whirl and cut overgrown grass when the machine is pushed forward. Reel mowers are easier to maneuver (move) than electric or gas mowers, and are much quieter than even an electric mower. They are also emissions free.

Reel mowers offer an environmentally friendly option to gasoline-powered mowers.

Go Green!

There are many ways to keep the yard looking nice without harming the environment. Below are tips to greening your yard.

Monitoring water use in the yard is one way to go green.

THE YARD

- If your family uses an automatic sprinkler system in the yard, be sure to monitor its use. Automatic sprinkler systems often turn on even after heavy rains, wasting water.

- Water plants in the morning to maximize your water use. When plants are watered in the afternoon, much of the water is **evaporated** by the sun.

- Soakers and drip hoses can also maximize water use. These hoses have tiny holes in them that let water seep out directly onto grass without losing excess water as evaporated spray. This can save up to 70 percent of the water you use with a regular hose.

- When you finish mowing the lawn, leave grass clippings on the lawn to keep your grass healthy. As these clippings **decompose** (break down), they add valuable **fertilizer** to your lawn, reducing the need for **synthetic** fertilizers.

- Raise the blades of your mower to about 3 inches (7.6 centimeters) to help keep weeds down in your yard. You also will not need to water your lawn as often if the grass is higher because taller grass is able to retain moisture better than short grass.

If you have a large backyard that needs constant watering, your family may wish to consider purchasing a rain barrel. These containers collect and store rainwater from roofs, which can then be used to water yards.

Look up information about **composting** food and yard waste. Composting is a process where leaves, food scraps, grass clippings, and yard waste are combined in a pile and left to decompose for several weeks. These substances eventually turn into a rich fertilizer full of nutrients for growing plants.

Drip hose attachments (above) can help reduce water use in the yard.

Composting food and garden waste (left) creates a rich fertilizer.

Rainwater barrels (below) catch rainwater from roofs, which can be used to water plants.

Taking Action

Section Summary

Governments around the world have passed laws to protect natural resources and encourage environmental responsibility.

State and local governments have also established laws to limit greenhouse gas emissions in order to help slow down global warming.

Businesses are working toward creating environmentally sound practices, such as enacting recycling programs and investing in renewable energy sources to balance out the amount of carbon dioxide they produce.

Individuals can help reduce the environmental impact of the goods by encouraging businesses and governments to set higher environmental standards for durable goods.

Government regulations in many countries require the regular testing of water and soil.

Government initiatives

Over the past few decades, governments around the world have increased efforts to reduce human impact on the environment and to encourage environmental responsibility from countries, businesses, and individuals. In 1997, world leaders gathered in Kyoto, Japan and passed an international protocol (statement of agreement) on actions to take to reduce **global warming**. The protocol, called the **Kyoto Protocol**, set limits for the amount of **carbon dioxide** and other **greenhouse gases** that countries can produce. Many of the world's countries, with the exception of the United States, have signed the Kyoto Protocol.

In the United States, the **Environmental Protection Agency (EPA)** and state governments have helped enforce and continually update important environmental laws, such as the Clean Air Act of 1970 and the Clean Water Act of 1972. The Clean Air Act **regulates** the wastes produced by industrial processes, by the burning of fuel, and by other sources. The Clean Water Act established laws to reduce or eliminate water pollution.

The EPA has also sought ways to encourage energy and water efficiency through the establishment of its **Energy Star** program. Energy Star promotes the manufacture and use of energy-efficient products, such as light bulbs, appliances, electronics, and office equipment. To qualify for an Energy Star label, a product must use between 10 to 50 percent less energy than regular models without compromising performance. Home appliances and electronics that meet Energy Star's efficiency guidelines bear the Energy Star logo so consumers can easily identify them. Canada, Australia, and the **European Union (EU)** also participate in the Energy Star program.

Since energy-efficient appliances are often significantly more expensive than standard appliances, many governments offer incentives for consumers, businesses, and building contractors to purchase Energy Star-rated appliances. The U.S. federal government offers tax credits for some Energy Star appliances that are at the highest end of the energy efficiency scale. Rebates (partial refunds) and sales tax credits are also sometimes offered on Energy Star appliances.

Recent government programs in Toronto, Canada, offer rebates to people who purchase Energy Star-rated washing machines. A program in the Yukon territory of Canada allows refunds for people who exchange old refrigerators for newer Energy Star models.

In an effort to reduce greenhouse gas **emissions**, the United Kingdom is considering taking measures to reduce energy use from durable goods. Government officials are working to ban plasma televisions, which require much energy to work and are therefore linked to greenhouse gas emissions. The British Prime Minister, Gordon Brown, has also announced his intention to outlaw the standby mode of most electronics sold in the United Kingdom.

In 2008, the European Union worked toward implementing a sweeping climate change reform treaty. The treaty will reduce carbon dioxide emissions from energy plants and reduce taxes on green durable goods so more people can afford them. The goal is to reduce carbon emissions by 2020 to below 1990 levels.

The Energy Star program helps consumers identify energy-efficient products.

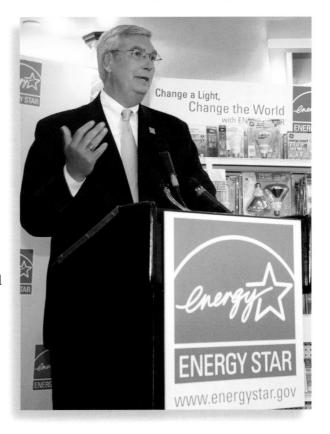

In some U.S. states, home-owners who install solar panels can sell back energy to electric power companies.

State and local governments

Some U.S. states have created laws to help counteract harmful pollution and the wasteful use of **nonrenewable resources.** These states offer tax incentives for people who purchase green durable goods or who use alternative forms of energy, such as **solar power,** to power their homes. Some states have outlawed the disposing of computer monitors and televisions into **landfills.** They have also created recycling programs for these durable goods.

In the United States, California has led the way in green initiatives. The California state government has passed laws similar to those passed by the European Union and plans to reduce the state's greenhouse gas emissions to below 1990 levels by 2020. California also allows homeowners that use **solar panels** for electricity to sell excess energy created by these panels back to the electric company to help cut down on the burning of **fossil fuels.**

City governments have also implemented green initiatives. By July 2008, 850 mayors of cities in the United States had signed a climate protection agreement that focuses on reducing greenhouse gas emissions in their cities.

Businesses

Rising energy costs, government regulations, and growing concern about global warming have all caused many businesses to take the environmental impact of their products seriously. Though there is still a long way to go until the majority of businesses are green, many have taken steps to reduce their **carbon footprint, conserve** fossil fuels, and recycle their products.

Many electronics businesses have created recycling and take-back programs for their used products. Some computer companies provide drop-off locations or discounted postage for the return of used laptops, printers, and monitors. A few computer companies will even pick up used office equipment for free. The equipment can then be recycled or donated to charity.

Many cell phone companies, as well as non-profit businesses, work to make sure you can donate your used cell phone to be recycled or reused. Most cell phone companies have drop-off locations for recycling at their stores, and some non-profits will collect your old phones to be **refurbished** or reused.

Some appliance manufacturers are working to reduce the amount of pollution their products release into the **atmosphere**. For example, refrigerator manufacturers are seeking ways to replace harmful chemicals from their machines with environmentally friendly materials. (See the "Closer Look" sidebar on page 19.)

Internationally, environmental responsibility is recognized at the World Economic Forum, a meeting among major governments of the world to discuss financial matters. Each year at this meeting, a list of the Top 100 Green corporations is released. This list shows companies that do such things as save large amounts of energy or work toward fighting pollution.

Individual action

Most businesses do not simply decide to go green. Rather, they respond to a rising call from customers to take environmental responsibility seriously. Here are three ways you can do more to reduce the impact of durable goods on the environment:

1. Know the environmental practices behind the durable goods you buy.
2. Share this knowledge with family and friends.
3. Participate in campaigns that encourage businesses and governments to set higher environmental standards for durable goods.

Purchasing energy-efficient appliances is one of many ways to reduce energy consumption.

Activities

MAKE A WATER-SAVING TOILET DEVICE

Introduction

Old toilets can be a source of much water waste. However, there are ways to reduce water use in your toilet without purchasing a new model. Follow the steps below to reduce the water consumption of your old toilet. Ask an adult to help you with this project to make sure that your water-saving toilet device does not interfere with the function of your toilet.

Materials:

- Empty 20-ounce plastic bottle with cap
- About 3 handfuls of pebbles or small stones (enough to fill half the bottle)

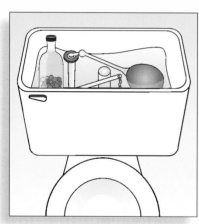

Directions:

1. Fill the bottle halfway with the small stones or pebbles. Make sure it is heavy enough so that it will not knock over easily. Add more stones or pebbles if necessary. Fill the rest of the bottle with water and screw on its cap.
2. Take the lid off of the toilet tank. Flush the toilet.
3. As the tank fills up with water, set the bottle inside the tank. Be sure that the bottle is not in the way of the float, which would cause it to interfere with the toilet's operation. After the tank is filled, the bottle will act as a water displacer. It will take up space in the tank so less water is needed to fill the tank.
4. Test your toilet to make sure it is flushing properly. If your toilet does not have strong enough flushing power to flush away waste, remove the water displacer.

TEST YOUR TOILET FOR LEAKS

Introduction

The bathroom is the source of the most water use in the home. Around the world, an estimated 27 percent of the water used by each home goes toward toilet use. Low-flow toilets can reduce water consumption by toilets, but we can also fix old toilets to make them more water efficient.

Leaky toilets can waste thousands of gallons of water a year, but it's not always easy to tell if a toilet has a leak. Try this simple activity to test your toilet for leaks.

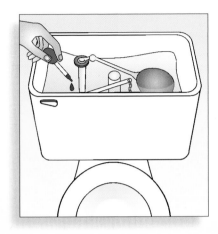

Materials:

- Bottle of food coloring

Directions:

1. Remove the lid to the tank of your toilet.
2. Take a bottle of food coloring and put five drops into the water in the tank.
3. Let the water sit for 30 minutes without flushing.
4. After the 30 minutes is up, check the toilet bowl. If you see the food coloring in the toilet bowl water, you know that you have a leak—and that it's time to call a plumber.

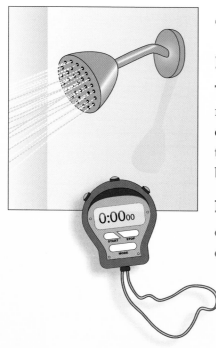

TEST YOUR SHOWERHEAD

Introduction

Though toilets are the biggest consumers of water in the bathroom, showers can also be a source of much water waste. As you can read in this book, many showerheads use more water than they need to. This quick, simple activity will tell you if it's time to buy a water-efficient showerhead or **aerator.**

Materials:

- 2-quart saucepan
- Stopwatch or watch with a second hand

Directions:

1. Take the saucepan and place it on the bottom of your bathtub or shower.
2. Turn on the shower, making sure the water is flowing at full force. Move the saucepan directly beneath the shower stream.
3. Using the watch, or by counting yourself, see how many seconds it takes to fill the pan. If it takes less than 12 seconds, your shower needs a low-flow aerator attachment. (These cost around $5.) Low-flow aerators can slow water loss to less than 3 gallons (11.35 liters) of water a minute.

RESEARCH PROJECT: E-WASTE

Introduction

As you can learn in this book, the amount of **e-waste** (electronic trash) throughout the world continues to grow. Conduct a research project to learn more about e-waste, its effects, and how people can work to reduce e-waste.

Directions:

1. Ask your teacher or school or public librarian to help you find information on e-waste. Together, come up with a list of things you'd like to find out about e-waste. Examples of such questions include:

- What are the environmental issues associated with e-waste?
- Which countries produce the most e-waste?
- What are the human hazards associated with e-waste?
- What are countries around the world doing to reduce e-waste?

2. Create a report that conveys important information about e-waste. The report could be in the form of a booklet, poster, collage, blog, podcast, or a combination of media. You may wish to include information about recycling electronics in your local community.

Glossary

aerator a showerhead or faucet attachment that mixes air into the water stream to reduce the amount of water being used.

atmosphere the mixture of gases in contact with Earth's surface and extending far above.

bio-based made primarily from plant and animal materials. Bio-based products are usually free of environmentally damaging substances.

biodegradable easily decomposed by living things.

brominated flame retardants (BFR's) chemicals that are used on some durable goods to help prevent them from catching fire.

by-product an additional product created in the manufacture of an object or substance.

carbon dioxide a colorless, odorless gas given off by burning and by animals breathing out.

carbon footprint the total amount of carbon dioxide given off by a particular human activity.

carbon monoxide a toxic, colorless, and odorless gas.

catalytic converter a device found in cars that reduces emissions from engine exhaust.

certify to declare something true or correct by an official spoken, written, or printed statement.

charcoal wood that has been heated to remove all water, making it easily flammable.

composting the process used to break down yard waste and food scraps into rich fertilizer for gardens and grass.

conserve; conservation to keep from harm or loss; the management, protection, and wise use of natural resources.

conventionally farmed grown using farming practices that include using human-made chemicals to grow plants.

crude oil the form of oil that comes directly out of the ground; petroleum.

decompose to break down; decay.

deforestation the destruction of forests.

disposable describes items that can be thrown away after use.

e-waste electronic trash such as cell phones, computers, and televisions.

emission an airborne waste product.

Energy Star a program run by the U.S. Environmental Protection Agency that rates energy and water efficiency of durable goods.

Environmental Protection Agency (EPA) the federal agency that works to protect the U.S. environment from pollution.

environmentalist a person who wants to preserve nature and reduce pollution.

European Union (EU) an economic and political organization that includes most of the countries of Europe.

evaporate; evaporation to change from a liquid or solid into a vapor or gas; the act or process of changing a liquid or a solid into vapor.

fertilizer a substance that helps plants to grow.

formaldehyde a colorless gas with a sharp, irritating odor.

fossil fuel underground deposits that were formed millions of years ago from the remains of plants and animals. Coal, oil, and natural gas are fossil fuels.

global warming the gradual warming of Earth's surface, believed to be caused by a build-up of greenhouse gases in the atmosphere.

greenhouse effect the process by which certain gases cause the Earth's atmosphere to warm.

greenhouse gas any gas that contributes to the greenhouse effect.

habitat the place where an animal or plant naturally lives or grows.

heavy metal a metal such as lead, mercury, or arsenic, which can collect in the tissues of organisms and is toxic to most living things.

hydrocarbon a chemical compound containing carbon and hydrogen.

incinerator a waste disposal facility that burns garbage.

industrialized country a country where historical wealth and advanced development contribute to a relatively high standard of living.

kilowatt a measure of electricity use. One kilowatt is 1,000 watts.

kilowatt-hour the work done by one kilowatt in one hour.

Kyoto Protocol the international agreement that set limits for the amount of greenhouse gases that countries can produce.

landfill a place where trash and other solid waste materials are discarded.

life span the time period from the creation of a material until its destruction.

nonrenewable resources resources that cannot be replenished once depleted, such as fossil fuels.

off-gassing the process by which chemicals evaporate over time.

organic produced by plant or animal activities; organic food is grown or raised without the use of synthetic chemicals.

ozone a form of oxygen gas.

particulate a tiny piece of solid material that floats in the air.

pesticide a poison that kills pests such as insects.

petroleum another name for the fossil fuel often called oil.

pollutant a single source of pollution.

propane a gas or liquid that comes from petroleum and is often used for outdoor grilling.

radiation energy given off in the form of waves or small particles of matter.

reclaimed wood old wood, such as from a demolished building, that is reused to make a new object.

refrigerant the liquid used in a mechanical refrigeration system.

refurbish to polish up again; renovate.

regulate; regulation to control by rule, principle, or system.

renewable resources natural resources, such as trees, that can be replaced after they have been harvested.

reproductive having to do with the ways in which organisms copy and perpetuate themselves.

sewage water that contains waste matter produced by human beings.

smelter a type of chemical factory in which metals are extracted from rocky material called ore.

smog a brown, hazy mixture of gases and particulates caused by exhaust gases released by automobiles and other users of fossil fuels.

solar panel a panel of tiny devices that convert the energy in sunlight to electric current.

solar power electricity that is created from the energy in sunlight.

sustainable any practice that adheres to principles of conservation and ecological balance.

synthetic human-made.

thermostat an automatic device for regulating temperature.

turbine a wheellike object that spins around and around.

ventilation exchanging inside air for outside air.

volatile organic compounds (VOC's) an unstable substance that breaks down over time and gives off small amounts of toxic gases.

Additional Resources

WEB SITES

Canadian Environmental Assessment Agency

http://www.ceaa-acee.gc.ca

Provides environmental assessments that contribute to well-informed decision making; supports sustainable development.

Energy Star

http://www.energystar.gov

A program of the U.S. Environmental Protection Agency; includes information on energy-efficient products and ways to save energy; includes a kids' page.

Energy Star—Canada

http://www.oee.nrcan.gc.ca/energystar

Canadian Web site for the Energy Star program.

Envirolink

http://www.envirolink.org/index.html

Includes articles and resources on a range of environmental issues.

Green Living Ideas

http://greenlivingideas.com

Provides numerous articles and information on reducing human impact on the environment.

Green Living Tips

http://www.greenlivingtips.com

Provides tips on how to "green" your lifestyle.

National Geographic

http://www.nationalgeographic.com

One of the leading environmental magazines; includes multimedia resources and a student page.

National Geographic Green Guide

http://www.thegreenguide.com

Includes numerous articles, charts, and tips on greening your lifestyle.

TUNZA

http://www.unep.org/Tunza

Part of the United Nations Environment Programme; a student-centered resource for environmental action.

WaterSense

http://www.epa.gov/watersense

A program of the U.S. Environmental Protection Agency; includes information on water-efficient products and ways to save water; includes a kids' page.

BOOKS

The Green Book: The Everyday Guide to Saving the Earth One Simple Step at a Time

by Thomas Kostigen and Elizabeth Rogers (Three Rivers Press, 2007)

Green Guide: The Complete Reference for Consuming Wisely by the Editors of Green Guide

(National Geographic, 2008)

The Complete Idiot's Guide to Green Living

by Trish Riley (Alpha Books, 2007)

It's Easy Being Green: A Handbook for Earth-Friendly Living

by Crissy Trask (Gibbs Smith Publishers, 2006)

Living Green: A Practical Guide to Simple Sustainability

by Greg Horn (Freedom Press, 2006)

Index